TRAVELS
THROUGH THE
FRENCH
RIVIERA

TRAVELS
THROUGH THE
FRENCH RIVIERA

AN ARTIST'S GUIDE
to the Storied Coastline,
from Menton to Saint-Tropez

Virginia Johnson

ARTISAN | NEW YORK

Library of Congress Cataloging-in-Publication Data

Names: Johnson, Virginia, 1972– author.
Title: Travels through the French Riviera : an artist's guide to the storied coastline, from Menton to Saint-Tropez / Virginia Johnson.
Description: New York : Artisan, a division of Workman Publishing Co., Inc., 2018.
Identifiers: LCCN 2017052459 | ISBN 9781579657376 (hardcover : alk. paper)
Subjects: LCSH: Riviera (France)—Description and travel. | Riviera (France)—Pictorial works.
Classification: LCC DC608.3 .J64 2018 | DDC 914.49/4048412—dc23
LC record available at https://lccn.loc.gov/2017052459

Cover illustration of Madeleine Castaing fabric by Virginia Johnson
Book and cover design by Raphael Geroni

For speaking engagements, contact speakersbureau@workman.com

Artisan books are available at special discounts when purchased in bulk for premiums and sales promotions as well as for fund-raising or educational use. Special editions or book excerpts also can be created to specification. For details, contact the Special Sales Director at the address below, or send an e-mail to specialmarkets@workman.com.

Published by Artisan
A division of Workman Publishing Co., Inc.
225 Varick Street
New York, NY 10014-4381
artisanbooks.com

Artisan is a registered trademark of Workman Publishing Co., Inc.

Published simultaneously in Canada by Thomas Allen & Son, Limited

Printed in China

First printing, May 2018

10 9 8 7 6 5 4 3 2 1

For my parents

CONTENTS

• • •

PREFACE

• • •

ONE LITTLE VILLA, PERCHED HIGH ON A
cliff in Saint-Jean-Cap-Ferrat, inspired me to write this book.

Villa Santo Sospir (see page 77) was the private home of
the Weisweiller family of Paris; famed artist Jean Cocteau
often stayed there, and his murals are frescoed all over the
walls. The villa exists today as it did then—with decorator Madeleine Castaing's exuberant textiles festooning the
windows, furniture, and floors, pictures of the family with
celebrated artists of the day scattered on tables, and elegant
French doors opening up to the view beyond. It embodies
all that is wonderful and sublime about the South of France
and everything the Riviera is known for: the light, the colors,
the art, the dazzling views, the sea, the absurd beauty, the
history, the good things in life. It exudes happiness.

I've been to the French Riviera a dozen times since I was
sixteen—as an art history student, with my parents, with
my husband, with my siblings, with friends. As I started
to write this book, I tried to pinpoint what it is about the
region that calls me back time and time again. Last May, I
set off with a map, my car, and a suitcase full of paints to
trace my favorite itinerary from Menton to Saint-Tropez,
going back to beloved haunts and discovering new ones. I
sketched the views of Nice from the hilltops of Cimiez (a
quiet, leafy neighborhood where Matisse once lived; see page
56), eighty-year-old bathing beauties on Plage des Sablettes,
chefs at the Grand-Hôtel du Cap-Ferrat, and the bocce play-
ers in Saint-Paul-de-Vence.

And what I found, besides the irrepressible beauty of the landscape, is that the art and the history seem so close here: some of the most well-known works of the twentieth century were wrought in these towns, and the stardust brushes off on you, too. It's everywhere. There's the Picasso Museum in the Grimaldi Castle in Antibes, where Picasso lived for six months in 1946; Matisse's Chapel of the Rosary in Vence, which he designed while living across the street in the 1940s; the Colombe d'Or hotel in Saint-Paul-de-Vence, whose owner traded paintings with artists in exchange for room and board, and where today masterpieces literally hang on the dining room walls.

My hope is that *Travels Through the French Riviera* will provide you with a loose guide to one of the most gorgeous coastlines on earth. All of my favorite places to visit (and sketch) are here—whether you go for three days or two weeks.

You don't need to be an artist to enjoy the Riviera, but if you are so inclined, I've included a list of the art tools that I love to bring with me when I travel (see page 192); or visit my go-to art supply store (see page 54).

Whether it's your first trip to the region or your fifteenth, I hope you will find something new to explore here. There's a warmth and beauty that washes over me every time I visit, filling me with a joie de vivre and returning me home more alive. This to me is the essence of the French Riviera.

I WAS IN MY EARLY TWENTIES WHEN I FIRST LAID EYES ON MENTON,

the so-called Pearl of France, the pretty little town where the sun shines 316 days a year and the classic Riviera coastline is the antithesis of the yacht-cluttered harbors of Monte Carlo, Cannes, and Saint-Tropez.

Its charms were undeniable. The locals were fashionable but not flashy. The Old Town was a car-free muddle of steep, narrow streets where getting lost was a simple pleasure. I navigated the alleys slowly, locating such staples as the *fromagerie*, the *boulangerie*, and boutiques that overflowed with racks of colorful bikinis and straw hats. Although most Old Town establishments catered to tourists (think pizza joints with red-checked tablecloths and bars touting live music on handwritten posters), I sensed that Menton was one of the few places on the Riviera where French tourists outnumbered the foreigners.

While Menton's Old Town remains the unassuming gem I discovered two decades ago, it's the glorious Plage des Sablettes that lures me back every time I'm on the Riviera. I never miss a chance to swim out from the sandy beach (one of a half dozen that hug Menton's coastline) to admire the picture-perfect backdrop: on one side, craggy mountains rise out of the sea, and on the other, the buildings of the Old Town are a blend of ochre, coral, pink, and gold, stacked atop the hill like a tiered cake. A single row of palm trees lines the boardwalk below.

Beyond the romantic Old Town alleys and the seaside views is a more practical side of Menton. Toward the main railway station and then off avenue de Verdun, you'll find stores that sell modern appliances (electric razors and toothbrushes, hair dryers, and more) that you may have forgotten at home. On backstreets, shoe vendors display stacks of sun-faded espadrilles and pharmacies are stocked with face creams made with natural ingredients and anti-aging superfoods, a staple in many a Frenchwoman's beauty regimen. And for those who yearn for an old-school retail experience, a visit to the stationery stores along rue Saint-Michel is a must.

Annonciade
Monastery

Rosary Path

Old
Château
Cemetery

bus
station

train
. station

Plage
des
Sablettes

Saint-
Michel
basilica

OLD TOWN

Salle des Mariages

food
market

Quai Napoléon III

Jean
Cocteau
Museum

beaches

Monaco
←

The buildings of Menton
radiate warmth in
corals, pinks, ochres,
and golds.

THE COLORS
of MENTON

• • •

Clay

Portrait pink

Sand

Putty

Gold

Apricot

Café

Rose

Naples yellow

Coral

Terra-cotta

Fuchsia

QUEEN VICTORIA IN MENTON

In 1882, the widowed Queen Victoria journeyed thirty hours to reach the French Riviera. It was a momentous trip that would lay the foundation for her travels for the next two decades. In the early years, the queen stayed in Menton. On her first trip, she brought her staff of one hundred, her bed, and a suite of furniture. On a subsequent visit, she bought a donkey and a small cart so that she could explore the area by herself. Queen Victoria continued to visit the region (later staying in Nice) until her death in 1901.

THE ANNONCIADE MONASTERY

Perched 738 feet above sea level, the Annonciade Monastery is a fair hike from downtown Menton, but the breathtaking views make the effort worthwhile. Built in the eleventh century, the monastery has been home to Capuchin monks and, more recently, the Sisters of the Annonciade. Most of the nuns have left, but the chapel remains open every day. Start from the roundabout on avenue de Sospel, just south of Menton's bus station. Taking the Rosary Path, you'll pass fifteen shrines along the way (Isabella of Monaco built these in the seventeenth century). From this point, it's a steep climb that takes about twenty minutes. At the top, expect to be overtaken by the sheer beauty of the monastery and the sense of calm that surrounds it. There are several benches under the shady esplanade where you can quietly take it all in. It's an inspiring place to pull out your sketchbook or to close your eyes and meditate.

THE OLD CHÂTEAU CEMETERY

From the Old Town, hike up to the Old Château Cemetery. Climb the steps from the beach to the Saint-Michel basilica and continue straight ahead. Turn right on rue du Vieux Château and take the steep walk upward from there. After catching your breath, enjoy the spectacular view of the Old Town and the sparkling Mediterranean beyond. Buried here are Russians, English, Germans, and French from the turn of the last century, many of them casualties of World War I.

THE JEAN COCTEAU MUSEUM

Jean Cocteau loved Menton and visited frequently when he was living in nearby Villa Santo Sospir. The mayor named him an honorary citizen for all of his contributions to the town, and to celebrate his life and work, Menton opened the Jean Cocteau Museum in 2011. Designed by renowned French architect Rudy Ricciotti, the building's striking façade of black-and-white structures is intended to represent the lightness and darkness of Cocteau's famously mercurial personality. Inside, you'll find almost a thousand works by Cocteau, the majority of which were donated by collector Severin Wunderman. Alongside Cocteau's graphic works are pieces by Matisse, Picasso, Chagall, and other Cocteau contemporaries who lived on the Riviera.

THE SALLE DES MARIAGES

Cocteau decorated the Salle des Mariages from 1957 to 1958. Since all weddings in France must be held at a town hall to be legally recognized, most Mentonnais pass through here at some point.

THE LADIES OF MENTON

One of the best things about Menton is the people-watching.
The women are so typically French—yet more relaxed and
cheerful than in other regions. They exude self-respect and
possess a certain resolute quality; they have been to the hair-
dresser, they have kept their shape (*gardez la forme!*), they
have their outfits all figured out—they are invincible. They
walk everywhere and take the time to greet one another and
catch up on the street.

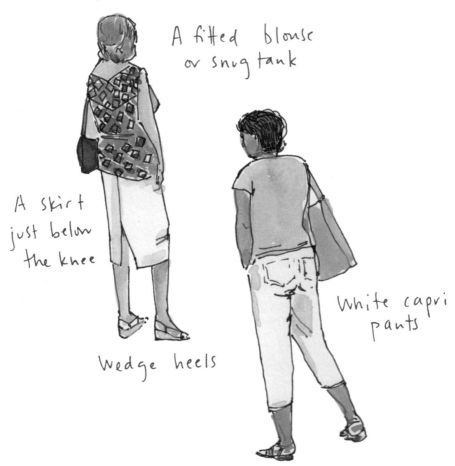

A fitted blouse
or snug tank

A skirt
just below
the knee

Wedge heels

White capri
pants

A deep tan

Salon-
styled hair

A chic handbag

BEACH SHOPPING

Menton offers many inexpensive shops for swimwear, tunics, and espadrilles.

Sun-bleached tunics from India in faded paisley prints (€45)

Swimming trunks from a rack outside an Old Town shop (€5)

Espadrilles found on one of the backstreets (€10)

AT THE BEACH

Menton has my favorite beaches in all the Riviera, and they're pretty low-key. Pull a tunic over your bathing suit and bring a straw mat or a towel, and a market bag for a visit to the food hall or an alfresco lunch. You don't need much to have the perfect beach day!

classic
market bag

Loose tunic

Leather
sandals

Grab a slice of pizza at a snack stand.

Cool off with an ice cream.

Octogenarians gathering in their bikinis for an early-morning dip

It's sunny here 316 days a year.

A DAY BY THE SEA

Menton's beaches are all beautiful. The spectacular views—with the Alps as a backdrop—make for great photos (and paintings). Depending on your preference, the farther east you go along the Promenade de la Mer, the more sandy and sheltered the beaches become. Here are a few tips for when you visit:

- Each of Menton's two train stations is a twenty-minute walk to Plage des Sablettes.

- September is a great month to go if you want to avoid the summer crowds.

- I prefer Menton's public beaches because I'm happy on my towel, but there are also private beaches where you can rent a lounger and an umbrella.

- There's plenty of parking.

- Wear your bathing suit to the beach. There are public bathrooms nearby for changing, but why bother? It's easiest to dry off in the sun and then just put your clothes back on.

- Bring a beach towel, sarong, or straw mat to lie on. You can also buy straw mats in the Old Town.

- You can find pizza, ice cream, and other snacks at restaurants lining the beach.

- There are outdoor showers near the edge of the beach to rinse the sand off your feet.

CITRON PRESSÉ

You can order a *citron pressé* in any café in
France, but it's especially lovely in Menton.
Blanketed by lemon trees, Menton supplied
citrus fruit to all of Europe for centuries, and
it's an important part of the town's identity. The
drink is tart and refreshing—not as watery and
sweet as lemonade—and you mix the compo-
nents yourself. Typically you're given a glass of
freshly squeezed lemon juice, some ice, a pitcher
of cold water, and sugar, so you can adjust the
sweetness to your liking.

It's easy to make at home, too. All you need is a glass of ice-cold water, juice from two or three lemons, and granulated sugar. Mix it all together, adding sugar to taste, and voilà!

A CHARMING MIX OF JOIE DE VIVRE AND OLD-WORLD GRIT,

N I C E

is the unofficial capital of the Côte d'Azur, a longtime retreat for artists and pleasure-seekers alike. The Greeks were the first to settle here (they named it "Nike"), then the Romans, the French, the Italians, and the French again. Many travelers consider it a launching-off point (the international airport and train station offer easy access to other parts of Europe), but I've always loved to spend a few days here and slow down to the pace of the locals. Nice's 350,000 residents make it the largest city on the French Riviera, and yet it has a decidedly small-town feel. At Monoprix, one of my favorite French department stores, cashiers *se font la bise* (kiss on the cheek) three times at shift changes. Bus drivers pick up passengers at undesignated stops and chat with them for the entire trip. Construction workers start the day with friends, over an espresso, at a local café. At noon, the streets fill with children and adults heading home for a two-hour lunch. Socializing is not considered frivolous here—it's an important part of life.

The city's setting is both strategic and scenic. It's positioned on the palm-tree-lined Bay of Angels, where you'll see Belle Époque buildings and a seaside promenade. To get a sense of the geography, first orient yourself to Nice's Old Town (Vieux Nice) on the east, bordered by Castle Hill (Colline du Château) and Nice Côte d'Azur Airport on the west. Place Masséna is a large, centrally located square where you can find the French retailer Galeries Lafayette and the start of a pedestrian zone that stretches four blocks, clear of vehicular traffic. It's lined with restaurants and cafés of all types. But be forewarned: most of them adhere to France's strict mealtime rules—breakfast from 8:00 to 9:00 a.m., lunch from noon to 2:00 p.m., and dinner from 7:00 to 9:00 p.m.—so you may search in vain for a midafternoon cappuccino.

train
station

Basilica
of Notre-
Dam

Monoprix

Promenade des Anglai

Bay of

Nice
Côte
d'Azur
Airport
↙

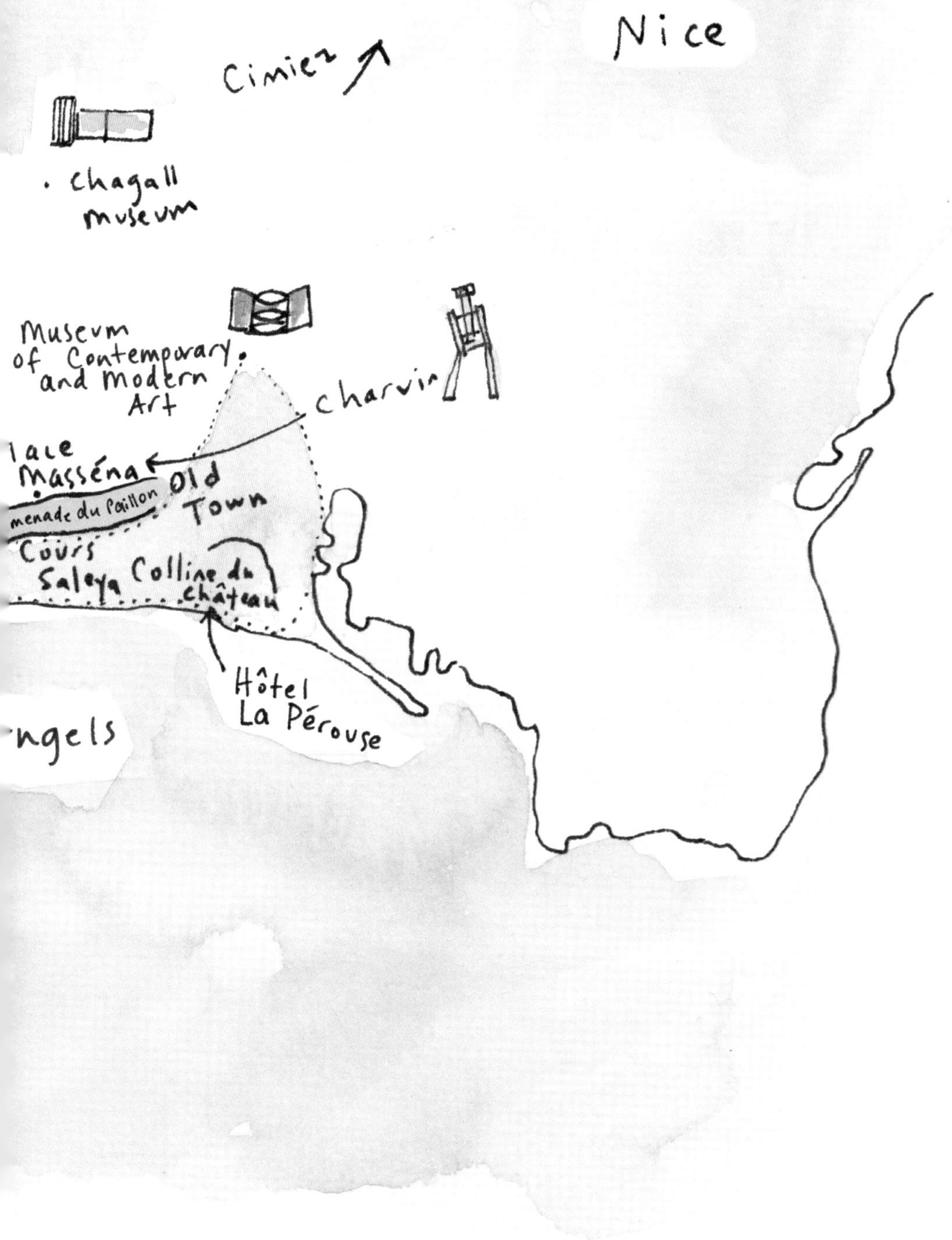

Nice

Cimiez ↗

chagall
museum

Museum
of Contemporary
and Modern
Art

charvin

lace
Masséna
menade du Paillon
Old
Town
Cours
Saleya
Colline du
château

Hôtel
La Pérouse

ngels

THE PROMENADE DES ANGLAIS

The moment you arrive in Nice, drop your bags and head straight to the Promenade des Anglais. Built at the prodding of the English aristocracy who spent their winters here, it follows the Riviera's longest waterfront, allowing visitors to walk uninterrupted for four miles.

There's bustling traffic on one side—Nice is a major city, after all. But what you give up in serenity, you get back in grandeur and scale.

Historic Belle Époque hotels line the route, with views that inspired the likes of painters Henri Matisse and Raoul Dufy. Posh seaside restaurants and private beaches may add an element of exclusivity, but for the most part Nice's pebbled beach is an egalitarian affair. Throw your towel down, claim your spot, and take in the iconic surroundings.

THE PROMENADE DU PAILLON

A thirty-acre green space brimming with 1,600 trees, 6,000 shrubs, and 50,000 perennials, the Promenade du Paillon has undeniably improved Nice's seafront. It extends from the Promenade des Anglais to the Museum of Modern and Contemporary Art, and effectively runs right through the heart of Nice. If you're with children, don't miss splashing around in the "water mirror" fountains.

THE MANY FACES OF NICE

Although 90 percent of Nice's population is French, the city's proximity to the rest of Europe and North Africa means there's great diversity in its people, shops, and eateries. Across the street from the Basilica of Notre-Dame, near the train station, you'll find a mosque, a Vietnamese restaurant, and a French butcher. The six largest immigrant groups are from Tunisia, Italy, Morocco, Algeria, Portugal, and Spain.

AN AFTERNOON IN THE OLD TOWN

For a true taste of this storied city, visit Vieux Nice, a triangle-shaped quarter on the east side of town, near the water. I'm never a fan of jostling among tourists, but I love walking the narrow cobblestone streets, shopping for souvenirs, eating ice cream, and retreating to a sunny patio to have a drink. Cours Saleya is a square that hosts a daily flower and produce market, as well as the Monday antiques market. Shops sell plenty of things to bring home with you. Most of the wares—chocolates wrapped in pretty boxes decorated with vintage illustrations of Nice, bottles of olive oil and sachets of dried lavender, fragrant Savon de Marseille (Marseille soap) in shades of South-of-France pink, raspberry, and lemon—are displayed in baskets that spill out onto the sidewalk. You'll find something for everyone on your list.

Hôtel La Pérouse is a discreet jewel, tucked into the cliff on the edge of the Old Town. Even if you're not staying there, dine at its restaurant, Le Patio, where delicious Mediterranean cuisine is served under the lemon trees on its beautiful terrace.

THE ANTIQUES MARKET

I never miss the chance to visit Nice's Monday antiques market. You may be on the hunt for a specific piece, or you may be happy just to poke around the stalls. There's furniture, loads of silverware, cloth napkins, champagne glasses, books, jewelry, vintage photographs, and old clocks. You never know what you will find. My friend and I once came across a few rolls of red-and-ecru-striped upholstery fabric propped up against a table, straight out of a Matisse still life; we bought enough to reupholster our dining room chairs. At a nearby stall, we found a pair of mugs with ceramic strainers and lids decorated with sprays of blue flowers for €10. When you've exhausted your energy, or your pocketbook, treat yourself to a *citron pressé* (see page 34) at one of the outdoor restaurants lining the square.

THE FLOWER MARKET

Fresh flowers are as necessary to French life as good espresso and croissants, and in Nice the place to get them is the Marché aux Fleurs. As you cross place Masséna and descend into Vieux Nice, toward Cours Saleya, it's hard not to spot the streams of people carrying large bouquets.

With hot, dry summers and mild winters, Nice's climate allows for plants to grow year-round. There's always plenty to choose from—roses, hibiscus, bougainvillea, lemons, lavender—displayed by dozens of vendors under their striped awnings. You'll want to buy everything you see.

One morning in early May, before boarding the train to Antibes, I stopped by the market to find hundreds of peonies displayed in deep buckets. The full, creamy white buds showed hints of pink and deep crimson. They were impossible to resist, especially since peonies weren't out yet at home. I scooped up ten and carried them around Antibes in a Pringles can filled with water. It was well worth the effort: they bloomed four days later when we arrived in Provence.

You can also find a fruit and vegetable market in Cours Saleya offering everything from melons, clementines, lemons, and artichokes to local olive oil and cheeses. Get there early for fresh baguettes and croissants. The vendors love to chat, so take the time to say *bonjour*. Bargaining is not customary here, and it's cash only.

CHARVIN

Follow in the footsteps of Cézanne and Bonnard and buy some paints from the renowned art supplier Charvin. This specialty shop has been mixing colors for Côte d'Azur artists since 1830. Its paint is still produced the old-fashioned way, in workshops in the nearby Var region. Cosmetics mills grind the pigment down to the finest grade possible, and clarified poppy oil binds it together. The result is brilliant, beautiful colors that can't be found anywhere else. The two hundred shades in Charvin's palette were developed specifically to reflect the unique light and colors of the Riviera.

Charvin's Nice store is decently sized and well stocked; don't be afraid to ask questions. I wanted to try oil painting, so the woman behind the counter guided me to bottles of linseed oil, brushes, cleaners, and rows of paints. Some paints are pre-boxed by color range, in sets of nine, and are truly irresistible. There are the greens (grass, may, olive, emerald, and a deep green-brown the color of tapenade), blues (turquoise, peacock, Prussian, and ultramarine), and pinks (ruby, coral, peach, and rose) that mirror the buildings of the seaside towns. This is the South of France in a box. These paints make fabulous gifts for the artist, or aspiring artist, in your life. A box costs about €48. There are also lovely notebooks with Charvin embossed in gold lettering that go for about €10 each.

At the back of the store, pure, unbleached, full-bodied linens are for sale. Purchase a piece to paint on, so you won't need to carry a stretched canvas around. They are primed with oil, not gesso, so your paint glides on beautifully. A half-yard (19 inches long by 78 inches wide) costs about €25. You can cut it into smaller pieces as needed and tape them onto a board later. (If you plan to be prolific, a ten-yard roll costs €550.) I rolled my piece into my backpack, with the top poking out, and set off to paint.

CIMIEZ

When I'm craving a bit of tranquility, I head north to the leafy hilltop neighborhood of Cimiez. Walk up boulevard de Cimiez, or take the number 15 bus to the Arènes/Musée Matisse stop. European kings and queens built winter palaces here in the nineteenth century, and ornate wedding-cake façades still line the route. After the market crash of 1929, most of them became luxury apartments.

Keep walking up boulevard de Cimiez, and eventually you will arrive at the Régina Palace (on your left), which was originally built as a hotel-residence to accommodate the needs of Queen Victoria and her staff. She visited each winter and occupied an entire wing. Henri Matisse maintained a vast apartment here from 1938 to 1943, combining two reception areas and filling the rooms with birds and paintings, before decamping to Vence for the duration of the war. The building is no longer a hotel, but you can still walk around the perimeter of the gardens and look up at the grand façade.

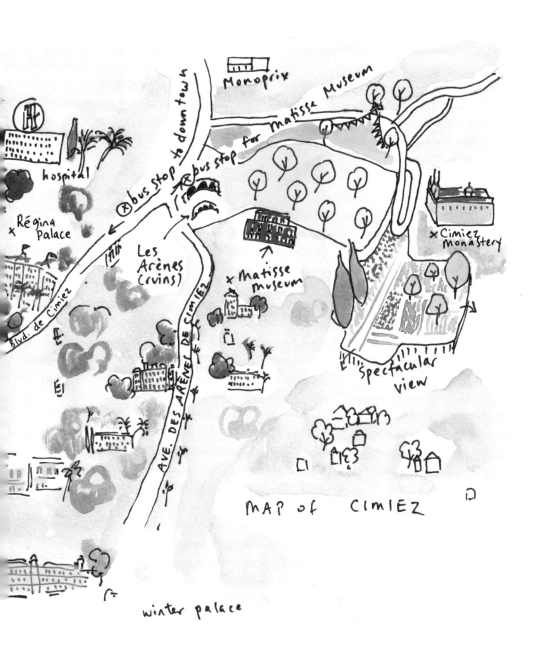

Monoprix

bus stop to downtown

bus stop for Matisse Museum

bus stop

hospital

Régina Palace

Cimiez Monastery

Les Arènes (ruins)

× Cimiez Monastery

× Matisse Museum

Blvd. de Cimiez

AVE. DES ARÈNES DE CIMIEZ

Spectacular view

MAP of CIMIEZ

winter palace

Farther up the boulevard, on your right, is the Arènes/Musée Matisse bus stop. Cross the street to the old Roman amphitheater, one of several ruins left from the area's once thriving Roman city. Then keep on toward the red-pink building that is the Matisse Museum.

THE MATISSE MUSEUM

Opened in 1963, the unassuming ten-room Matisse Museum is housed in a seventeenth-century Genovese-style residence across from the Régina Palace. The museum does not showcase Matisse's most famous pieces, but it offers many lovely works spanning his life, and ephemera such as chairs and objects he depicted in his paintings. You can learn much about his process and about who he was as a genius and a human being here.

The museum is also home to some personal letters, including one he wrote after his mother gave him his first box of paints when he was twenty-one: "From the moment I had this box of color in my hands, I felt that it was my life . . . it was the great attraction, the kind of found paradise in which I was free to do anything, alone, tranquil."

There are many unfinished works on display at the museum that provide rare insight into Matisse's decisions, what he was drawn to, and what he left out. He took time to develop his signature style; he struggled at times to remain relevant, painting pretty models and still lifes when the art world was marching in a different direction.

There are sculptures cast in bronze, odalisques, still lifes, pencil sketches, and paintings. *Figure Endormie* is one of my favorite pieces here. Upstairs you can see Matisse's cutouts. They are all housed in a wooden display rack made by his son. The "rejects" are now available to us to flip through and touch through plastic sleeves. There's no need to elbow through crowds to peer at carefully pinned arrangements on a faraway wall. They're here, painted and cut, as if anyone could make them.

One of the museum's gems is a model of the Chapel of the Rosary (see page 150) that Matisse constructed of wood and cardboard and painted with blue zigzags. Photography is forbidden at the museum, so I made this sketch.

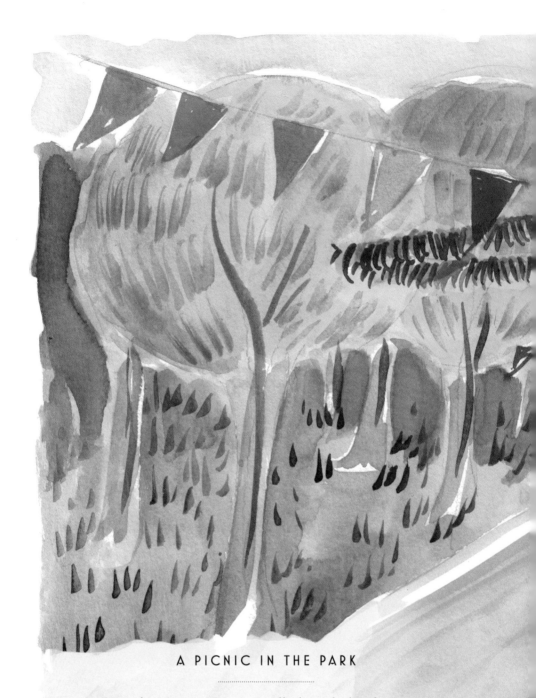

A PICNIC IN THE PARK

From the Matisse Museum, walk through the olive groves in the park to the Cimiez Monastery. There are no restaurants in Cimiez, so this is a good place to bring a picnic. Alternatively, try to catch the snack stand when it's open, or walk to the Monoprix a few blocks north and buy a quiche.

THE CIMIEZ MONASTERY

A treasure founded by Benedictine monks in the ninth century and surrounded by stunning gardens, the Cimiez Monastery offers one of the best views of Nice—the ocean, the terra-cotta rooftops, and the city below. As you walk through the gates, on your right you'll find a profusion of roses in fuchsia, vermilion, peach, and coral; to your left are serene trees in sculptural shapes and several stone paths. Keep walking to the pergola, an ideal spot to take in the view or to paint—you may even see a wedding or two. You could easily spend the whole afternoon here.

At the other end of the monastery, on the side opposite the gardens, is the cemetery where Matisse and Dufy are buried.

The grand gated entrance to
the monastery gardens

View from the Cimiez Monastery
in the rain

THE CHAGALL MUSEUM

After leaving the Cimiez Monastery, on your way back down-town, make sure to visit the Chagall Museum. Inaugurated in 1973, the museum contains one of the largest Chagall collections—four hundred paintings, drawings, gouaches, and pastels—and is centered around his "Biblical Message," a series of seventeen paintings created between 1962 and 1967.

There's a lovely garden, designed by Marc Chagall himself, and an outdoor café.

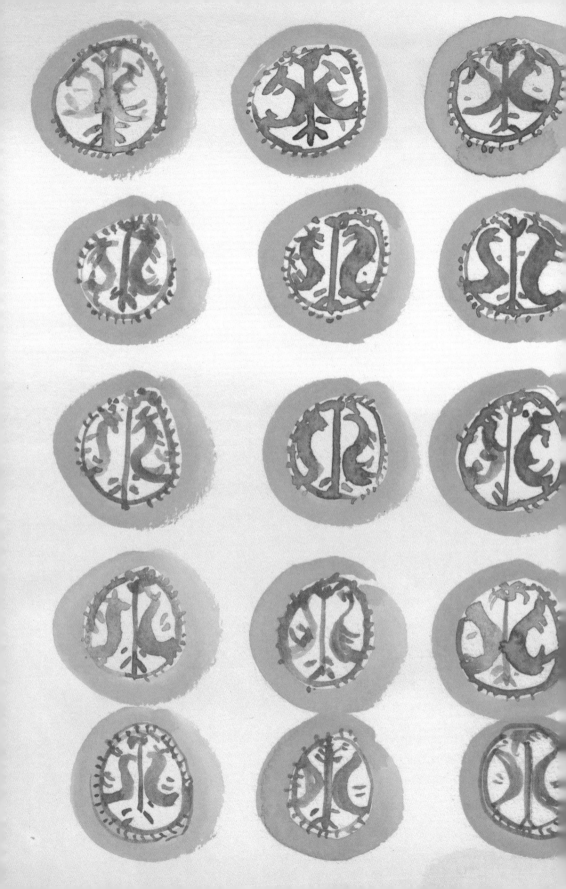

Saint-Jean-Cap-Ferrat

DOTTED WITH VILLAS IN THE BELLE ÉPOQUE, ART DECO, AND RENAISSANCE STYLES,

SAINT-JEAN-CAP-FERRAT

personifies the grandeur of the French Riviera. The sumptuous nine-mile promontory juts dramatically into the Mediterranean Sea just east of Nice, with an upper-crust charm that once lured the likes of Elizabeth Taylor, Richard Burton, and Gregory Peck. Hidden behind tall hedges and surrounded by perfectly manicured gardens, villas that once belonged to the Hollywood elite are now the summer homes of the ultrarich.

At the turn of the last century, this windswept peninsula had scrubby, rocky terrain, but that changed when European aristocrats arrived and started cultivating the landscape. In the late 1800s, King Leopold II of Belgium acquired several large properties (one of which was later sold and became the Grand-Hôtel du Cap-Ferrat; see page 92), and Béatrice Ephrussi de Rothschild bought her parcel in 1905 (see page 100). Eventually, Cap Ferrat grew dense with the lush tropical vegetation you see today, and the well-heeled inhabitants amassed real estate that now ranks as the second-most expensive in the world after Monaco.

But don't be intimidated by Cap Ferrat's five-star reputation: day travelers can enjoy its beauty as well. Take the road into its main port town of Saint-Jean-Cap-Ferrat (often referred to as Saint-Jean) and you'll find that it has a small-town feel. Fishing boats docked alongside yachts and a handful of low-key cafés and restaurants cater to all tastes and budgets. Mass tourism can't quite get there (the roads in and out are too narrow for huge coach buses, and there's no train station), which means the best ways to take in the million-dollar views are by car or on foot. My favorite way to explore the cape is on foot, hiking the coastal path.

Le Sentier du Littoral, or coastal path, is one of the most stunning walks of the Riviera. If you're coming straight from Nice, bus number 81 can take you from the Promenade des Arts directly to the town of Saint-Jean-Cap-Ferrat—about a thirty-minute ride—for €1.50.

Villa Ephrussi

town of Saint-Jean-Cap-Ferrat

Villa
Santo
sospir

Grand-Hôtel du
Cap-Ferrat

lighthouse

Cap Ferrat

HIKING AROUND CAP FERRAT:
LE SENTIER DU LITTORAL

The southern tip of the peninsula, with the lighthouse in the background, is your view as you leave town for the coastal path.

Fortify yourself with a coffee at one of the cafés around the port. Then head out to avenue Jean Mermoz; keep straight until the dead end, then turn right onto avenue Claude Vignon. This road leads to chemin de la Carrière on your left, which is the start of the trail. It will take you all the way around the cape. There are no places to buy water, however, so be sure to bring some along, and a hat.

The terrain is quite rugged. On one side is the sea, its waves crashing onto the rocks, and on the other a steep bank. Beware: there is no safety railing, and it's best not to bring very small children. Along the way, on your right you'll see stunning villas. Their gardens are meticulously manicured, full of cypresses and pine forests typical of the surrounding landscape. You'll also pass several beaches and hidden coves, and the legendary Grand-Hôtel du Cap-Ferrat, with its funicular running up the cliffs. The path is relatively flat, and it takes about forty-five minutes to reach the lighthouse, a distance of just under two miles. I usually stop here, but you could continue around the west side for another hour and a half (about four more miles). Climb the steps to the lighthouse, take chemin du Phare to avenue Jean Cocteau, and you'll find the enchanting Villa Santo Sospir at number 14.

Villa Santo Sospir

The courtyard, with a
mosaic by Cocteau

VILLA SANTO SOSPIR

Hidden behind tall umbrella pines, high up on a cliff, Villa Santo Sospir feels like the end of the earth. The villa has sweeping views of Villefranche and Nice and is positioned at the very tip of Cap Ferrat. Walk through the gates, along a shady path, inhale the pine scent, and step through a mosaic-tiled courtyard to the front door of the house. The villa itself is not grand, and that's part of its allure. It's decidedly non-chalant; glamorous but not drawing attention to itself, a beauty that just can't help being so beautiful. There are four bedrooms, a living and dining area, two bathrooms, a small kitchen, and a terrace. Terra-cotta pots overflow with nasturtium and hibiscus. Sentimental objects are scattered around the tables. It's a magical place.

Owned for the past seventy years by the Weisweiller family of Paris, Villa Santo Sospir is known today for its most famous houseguest, Jean Cocteau, who painted murals all over the walls. But there's much more to the story.

During World War II, Alec Weisweiller, a Jewish American banker and millionaire, and his glamorous young wife, Francine, the daughter of a well-to-do jeweler, fled Paris to the south to escape the Germans. He promised to buy her any house she wanted if they survived the war. In 1945, he made good on his promise and bought her this villa.

But Alec was more interested in his life in Paris, and for the most part Francine was free to live her life as she pleased, on the Côte d'Azur. She was attracted to the bohemian life of the resident artists and poets—she was friends with Coco Chanel and Yves Saint Laurent—and became Cocteau's patron after bailing him out during the filming of his movie *Les Enfants Terribles* (the lead actress, Francine's cousin, introduced them). Soon after, Francine invited Cocteau to the villa for a holiday, and he ended up staying for ten years. They were very close—inseparable—although their relationship was platonic; Cocteau's young boyfriend, Édouard Dermit, also lived with them. They filmed movies there (including the thirty-five-minute *La Villa Santo Sospir*, which shows off the villa's grounds) and entertained constantly with a who's who of the Riviera: Marlene Dietrich, Greta Garbo, and Pablo Picasso were regular guests.

Francine and Alec's daughter, Carole, was eight when her mother met Cocteau, and she spent her holidays with them in Cap Ferrat. The rest of the year she lived in Paris, raised by nannies, so to her the villa was a happy, joyful place: "I discovered the real family life I had dreamt of . . . where parents and children lived together with the same hours and on the same floor."

Cocteau, Francine, Picasso, and Picasso's then-girlfriend, Jacqueline Roque, c. 1955

One of Cocteau's
many frescoes.
Cocteau referred to
the house as a
"tattooed villa."

Carole
Weisweiller

The living room is the first room you see, just past the foyer, with French doors on the far wall opening to the Mediterranean Sea. It's cozy and personal, furnished with wicker armchairs, tropical fabrics, family pictures, and vases filled with flowers. Cocteau's large Apollo mural extends outward from the fireplace to cover three walls.

A friend of Francine's, the renowned French decorator Madeleine Castaing, was engaged to decorate the villa. She moved in rarefied circles and counted among her friends many famous artists, including Chagall, Cocteau, Picasso, and Modigliani (her portrait by Soutine hangs in the Metropolitan Museum of Art). Her eclectic mix of jungle prints, bamboo furniture, leopard-print rugs, and Indian chintzes defines the villa as much as—or, I would say, more than—Cocteau. She knew how to design spaces for leisure and good living that were elegant but not pretentious, choosing beautiful objects that were seemingly thrown together without effort. Local artisans from Fréjus were employed to craft the blinds by hand, bamboo furniture was made to measure and shipped in from Java, and a pair of antique eighteenth-century peacock beds were found in Nice.

Madeleine Castaing

Blue chintz upholstery

Madeleine Castaing
palm-frond fabric

Carole's bathroom in
Castaing's signature colors:
blue and green

A leopard-print rug

Madeleine
Castaing trellis
and bamboo fabric

THE VILLA TODAY

There have been no renovations and very few changes made to the villa since the 1950s. A worn rug or two has been replaced, but the fabrics, while a little tattered, are intact, and the original drapes, though long ago faded, are still hanging.

Several years ago, Menton's Cocteau Museum urged Carole to open up the villa to the public. Since Francine had died in 2003, Carole had maintained the villa as a holiday home and used it when she was not in Paris. She had always been an advocate for Cocteau's legacy and agreed to allow small tours during the months she was not staying there. This is why the villa feels so alive—it has been a family home all this time.

Éric Marteau is the current caretaker of the house and gives wonderful tours in both French and English, full of colorful anecdotes about the villa and its guests over the years. He should know—he was Francine's nurse in the years before she died and maintains a strong relationship with the Weisweiller family today.

In 2016, Carole sold the villa, but the new owners plan to keep it open to the public. At the time of this writing, it was still possible to schedule a tour of the house.

Éric Marteau

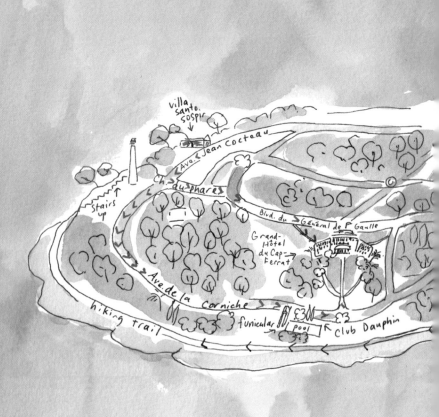

WALKING TO THE
GRAND-HÔTEL DU CAP-FERRAT

It's a ten-minute walk from Villa Santo Sospir to the Grand-Hôtel du Cap-Ferrat (follow the red arrows in the map above). Take avenue de la Corniche, and on the left you'll see the hotel gates and a central walkway leading up to the building.

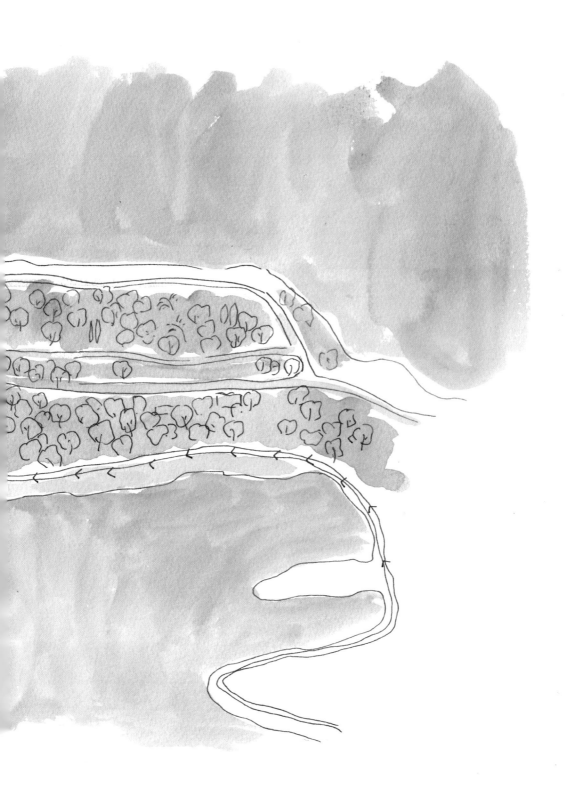

THE GRAND-HÔTEL DU CAP-FERRAT

Built in 1908, the Grand-Hôtel du Cap-Ferrat (not to be confused with its equally decadent neighbor, Hotel du Cap-Eden-Roc on Cap d'Antibes) was a winter escape for well-to-do Europeans, and favored by the likes of Winston Churchill, Pablo Picasso, Frank Sinatra, and Elizabeth Taylor. In the late 1920s a group of writers asked the owners to stay open for the summer to host their guests, and a new trend was born. The hotel is now part of the Four Seasons hotel group.

The hotel is surrounded by seventeen acres of stunning gardens and fronted by a meticulous lawn leading down toward the sea. As you wander through the garden paths, under a canopy of Aleppo pines, holm oaks, and olive trees, you'll pass by masses of camellias, lilies, and jasmine, just some of the four hundred species lovingly maintained by eight year-round gardeners. Although the hotel is set back from the water, you can cross the road at the foot of the gardens and descend to the seaside Club Dauphin via funicular. Here you will find an Olympic-sized saltwater infinity pool, built in 1939, and a poolside restaurant. The more adventurous can dive off the nearby cliffs and swim in the sea.

With its lush landscaping and waterside perch, this hotel is considered one of the most iconic on the French Riviera.

The hotel's octogenarian swimming instructor, Pierre Gruneberg, is a living legend. He gave swim lessons to Picasso, Cocteau, the Kennedy children, Brigitte Bardot, and Ralph Lauren, and his "Golden Book" is filled with notes and sketches from those famous guests. He still begins each day with a swim to the lighthouse and calls the hotel paradise on earth: "I go to work in a pair of trunks and a Mexican sun hat." A private lesson is €98.

Pierre Gruneberg

Today, the hotel is a hub during the Cannes Film Festival and continues to be a popular celebrity getaway. A decadent cream-and-white Art Deco–style renovation was completed in 2009, enveloping the interiors in soothing Calacatta marble, crystal chandeliers, and heavy silk drapery. Fabrics were sourced from storied French textile houses Manuel Canovas and Pierre Frey. A private villa with its own pool is available for just over €5,000 per night. Those on a more modest budget can enjoy a cucumber julep (made with freshly picked herbs from the hotel's aromatic garden) on the terrace for €26 and wander the gardens for free.

The hotel staff is warm and friendly, and dressed to the nines—they look like they are wearing dresses just flown in from Paris.

Michèle

Aurore

Grand Hôtel du Cap

L'Afternoon Tea
de 15:00 à 18:00

Grand-Hôtel Tradition
Afternoon Tea .... 35 €

Grand-Hôtel Célébration
Afternoon Tea ...... 45€

Grand-Hôtel Champagne.....
Afternoon Tea ...... 45 €

Grand-Hôtel Prestige
Afternoon Tea ..... 145€

Guillaume

The chefs take
a break near
Club Dauphin.

MY FAVORITE GREENS

• • •

Schmincke watercolor
in Prussian Green

Schmincke watercolor
in May Green

Schmincke watercolor
in Sap Green

Schmincke watercolor
in Hooker's Green

koi watercolor in
Yellow Green

Winsor + Newton
gouache in Permanent
Green Middle

koi watercolor in
Deep Green

Winsor + Newton
gouache in Sap Green

Winsor + Newton
gouache in Permanent
Green Light

VILLA EPHRUSSI

Farther up the coast, in 1905, Béatrice Ephrussi de Rothschild began work on a spectacular yellow ochre villa from the ground up, in the style of an Italian palazzo. While the setting was idyllic—on the west side of Cap Ferrat, looking out over both the Bay of Villefranche and the Bay of Ants (baie des Fourmis)—the terrain was unfavorable. She hired the best landscape architects in Europe and enlisted hundreds of Italian workers to dynamite and relevel the rocky ground, and then spent another seven years planting the gardens around what is now known as Villa Ephrussi.

In 1912, Béatrice moved in. The French formal gardens fronting the villa were ready, but she continued to work on the remaining ones. She even had the gardeners use life-sized cardboard pyramids and strips of silver fabric to represent cypress trees and ponds, so that she could get the placement exactly right.

Most of the themed gardens that you can stroll through today—including the Japanese, Florentine, Stone, Exotic, Rose, Provençal, and Sèvres—were created later, after Béatrice's death. In her will, she left the villa to the Académie des Beaux-Arts, and it hired landscape architect Louis Marchand to continue Béatrice's vision.

The property was abandoned during World War II, and the grounds fell into disrepair. Marchand was brought in again to restore the building and gardens, which included painting the villa in the iconic pink hue that is seen today.

The interiors are beautiful. Béatrice had luxurious tastes, and she decorated her rooms with a mix of rococo and neo-classical furniture, Chinese silks, and rugs from the Palace of Versailles. Some of the panels in her bedroom were painted, in the eighteenth century, by Marie Antoinette's artist. The Rothschild family traded silks extensively with China, and Béatrice's tiny shoes are displayed here as evidence of her foot-binding practice. The dressing room showcases her love of textiles, including Mandarin robes and silk gowns.

Béatrice was a serious art collector, and the walls of the villa are filled with her treasures. She installed Venetian murals by Giambattista Tiepolo, pastoral rococo scenes by François Boucher, and pen-and-ink washes by Jean-Honoré Fragonard.

Although the site is close to Villa Santo Sospir and the Grand-Hôtel du Cap-Ferrat, I recommend devoting a full day in your itinerary to this villa.

THE TEAROOM

Enjoy a light lunch of salad or a vegetable tart followed by tea on the terrace of what used to be
Béatrice's dining room. Through floor-to-ceiling
gold-scalloped windows, look out at the incredible
view of the Bay of Villefranche.

THE ROSE GARDEN

There are hundreds of fragrant varieties in the rose garden in all shades of pink, white, and cream; May, June, and July are the best months to view the garden in full bloom.

Béatrice entertained frequently in her gardens with poetry readings and ballet performances—legend has it that one evening, renowned ballerina Anna Pavlova danced to Chopin in the moonlight. Béatrice also kept her own private zoo with flamingos, monkeys, and antelopes.

THE EXOTIC GARDEN

The exotic garden is full of succulents and giant cacti, as well as many species of agave, aloe, and figs. You may bring watercolors and paint in the gardens if you inform the guard at the entrance.

Saint-Paul-de-Vence

IF YOU NEED A BREAK FROM
THE HUSTLE AND BUSTLE OF
THE COAST, HEAD INLAND TO

SAINT-PAUL-
DE-VENCE.

A mere twenty minutes' drive northwest of Nice, this medieval hilltop village feels like a different world. It's perhaps best known for the artists who visited in the 1900s. Matisse, Braque, Calder, Miró, and Chagall, to name a few, were attracted to its light and beauty, and to the sympathetic proprietor of the Colombe d'Or hotel, who gave them a place to stay. Today, Saint-Paul may be more affluent than it was a hundred years ago, but it's far from showy. This way of life is open to all; it seems to say, "Welcome." It's just a high-end version of what goes on in French towns everywhere.

The journey from the coast is a smooth transition from the glitter of the Riviera to artistic serenity. As you turn off the autoroute, you'll start climbing north into the hills, winding through one roundabout after another, past pizzerias and garden stores selling oversized terra-cotta pots. The air becomes noticeably purer, the villas more private, and the grounds more dense with cypress and olive trees. Follow the winding road until you crest at Saint-Paul-de-Vence, one of the oldest medieval towns of the French Riviera. Its modest permanent population of four thousand swells in the summer months. Base yourself here for a few days any time of year and you'll be able to experience the glorious early mornings and late evenings when most tourists have left for the day.

It's hard not to be awestruck by the magnificence of Saint-Paul's ancient ramparts. Built in 1537 at the request of King François I, the wall protectively circles the pretty cobbled streets and stone houses of the village. Before you pass through the gates, however, take time to explore the main street just outside the wall. There's a Fragonard store, a pharmacy, a newspaper kiosk, a fruit seller, a café, and a bocce court. Cars aren't permitted inside the village, but there's a ten-level subterranean parking lot nearby at the Espace Sainte-Claire. The shop at the top of the stairs sells large bags of lavender and laurel oil soaps.

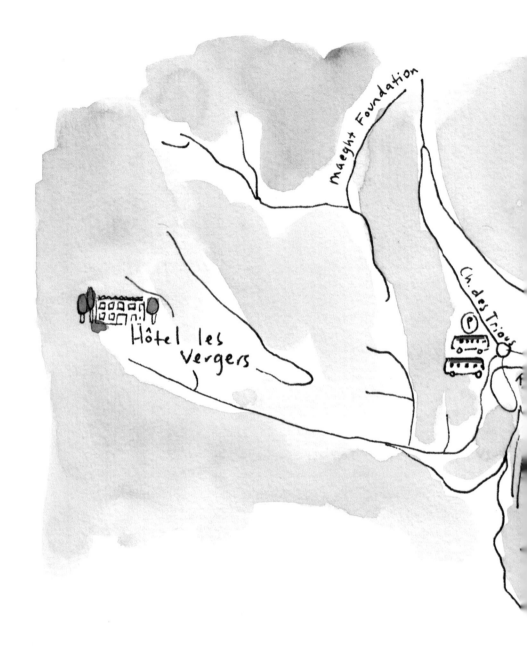

Hôtel les Vergers

Maeght Foundation

Ch. des Trious

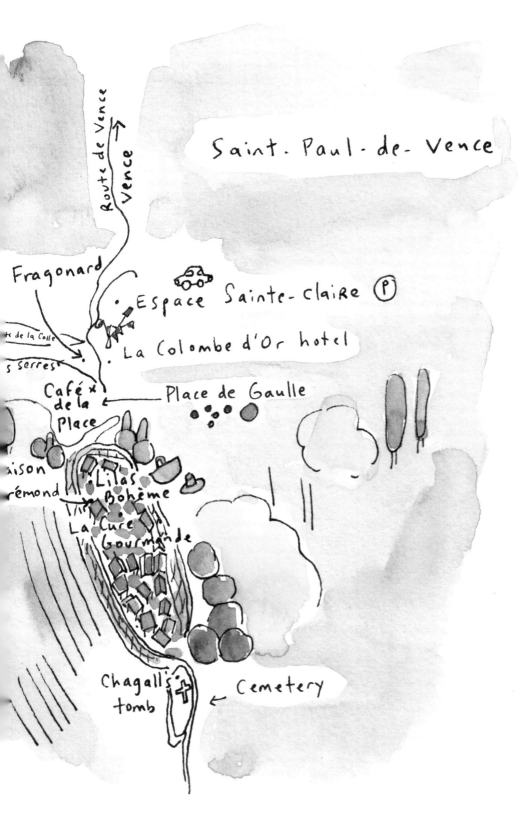

Saint-Paul-de-Vence

Route de Vence
Vence

Fragonard

Espace Sainte-claire Ⓟ

t de la Colle

s serres

La Colombe d'Or hotel

Café
de la
Place

Place de Gaulle

aison
rémond

Lilas
Bohème

La Cure
Gourmande

Chagall's
tomb

← Cemetery

BOCCE AND
PEOPLE-WATCHING

Local men play bocce (the French version is called *pétanque*) in place de Gaulle, the square outside the village walls, while tourists relax at the Café de la Place. This is a great spot to people-watch and enjoy a croque monsieur.

THE FRUIT SELLER

A lot of interesting characters live and work in Saint-Paul. There's a little stand set up near the wash station, just a few feet away from the entrance to the Colombe d'Or, with seasonal fruit, vegetables, and colorful flowers on offer. I spent an hour one day sketching the fruit seller crisscrossing the square to clean her buckets.

LA COLOMBE D'OR

Although La Colombe d'Or is one of the most famous hotels on the Riviera, its appearance (particularly its understated façade) personifies the simple-chic style of Saint-Paul. In the 1920s and '30s, Paul Roux, the founder of the hotel, offered room and board to struggling artists in exchange for their paintings. The hotel's terrace and bar in turn became a hub for some of the greatest thinkers and artists of the twentieth century. Today, the hotel possesses an outstanding private collection that includes works by Braque, Delaunay, Léger, Miró, Matisse, Picasso, and Chagall. The most extraordinary part is that these masterpieces are hung casually on the dining room walls and throughout the hotel's common areas. There's even a Calder mobile outside by the pool.

One of my favorite places in Saint-Paul is the hotel's restaurant, especially its exterior courtyard. It is full of fig trees and rosebushes, shaded by a canopy of white umbrellas. Friendly, attentive waiters make you feel at home. You don't have to stay at the hotel to eat here, but be sure to book a table months in advance.

Despite its rich history, La Colombe d'Or, with only twenty-five rooms, is still a family-owned *auberge*, lovingly cared for by Paul's grandson François Roux and his wife, Danièle. The owners take pride in the hotel's low-key, secluded atmosphere. Interiors are outfitted simply with white stucco walls, terra-cotta floors, and humble wooden furniture. The amenities of high-end Riviera hotels are notably absent (there's no spa, no state-of-the-art TV), but for those who want the personal touch of a traditional Provençal inn and a chance to experience a part of history, this is the place. It's not completely out of reach, either: prices range from €250 to €430 per night, depending on the season.

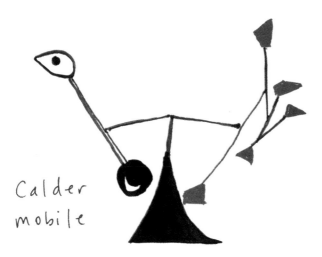

Calder mobile

The menu famously has not changed in fifty years. Dinner will cost you about €80 per person.

Le petit pot de Caviar 340 €

Le Foie gras de Canard 89€

Les Hors d'Oeuvre Colombe d'Or avec sa Charcuterie

Le Panier de Crudités et sa terrine 19 €

Potage aux Légumes 10 €

Melon-Jambon de Parme 14 €

Bouquet de Crevettes 27€

Saumon fumé sauvage de Suède 27€

La Cassolette d'Escargots de Bourgogne 19 €

You might be surprised that the panier de crudités comes with whole radishes, celery stalks, and artichokes.

WALKING THROUGH SAINT-PAUL

Year-round (and in the summer months especially), the village is overrun by tourists flocking to Saint-Paul's countless art galleries. I'm not a big fan of the art that's for sale, but if you're looking for presents to bring back home, you're bound to find something in one of the village boutiques. La Cure Gourmande offers chocolates and sweets in pretty tin boxes; Maison Brémond stocks delicious pestos and tapenades. For block-printed tunics, scarves, and straw bags, go to Lilas Bohème. It's a pleasant stroll through the narrow cobblestone streets with plenty of places to stop for an ice cream, a slice of pizza, or a drink.

THE CEMETERY

At the southern end of the village is the cemetery, perched on the edge of the medieval walls with spectacular views on three sides. There's a pea-gravel path, potted geraniums, lilies and carnations, and a little church from the twelfth century that once marked the center of town. Chagall, who lived in Saint-Paul-de-Vence for almost twenty years, is buried here, as are Aimé and Marguerite Maeght, alongside their eleven-year-old son, Bernard (see page 127).

Embroidered floral tunic

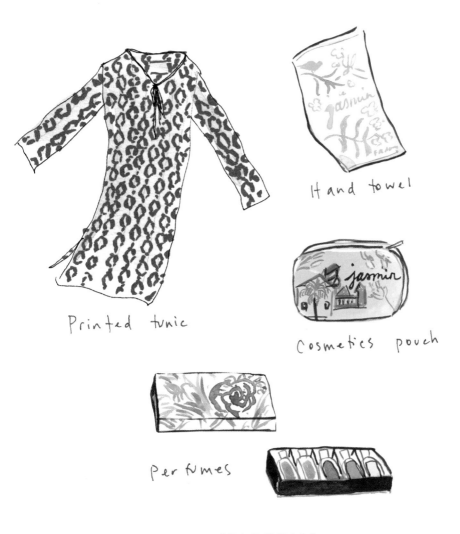

Printed tunic

Hand towel

Cosmetics pouch

Perfumes

FRAGONARD

For more inspired shopping, leave the Old Town and visit Fragonard on the main street. I can spend a whole afternoon in this one shop! Fragonard is primarily a Provençal perfume maker but offers much more. There are tunics with embroidered yellow flowers, caftans with tomato-red prints, and ruffled girls' sundresses. You'll be charmed by the pretty perfume boxes with watercolor illustrations and totes, handkerchiefs, and embroidered travel sacks. Of course, the perfumes are heavenly too.

THE MAEGHT FOUNDATION

Obscured by the hills and pines surrounding Saint-Paul, just a short walk from the main square, is the extraordinary Maeght Foundation. Cannes art dealers Aimé and Marguerite Maeght created this space in 1964 to show contemporary art in an entirely new way: art and architecture integrated together in nature. The Maeghts were adamant that this was not a museum, that it was not just a building with paintings inside, but a place where art and structure were one and the same.

They commissioned their artist friends to create site-specific works for their project, and some of the best-known artists of the era signed on. Miró installed a sculpture garden at the entrance populated by his colorful characters, and collaborated with the architect on the building's structure; Braque created a mosaic pool for the inside patio; and Giacometti carved out a series of lonely figures that roam around an interior courtyard. I find the temporary exhibits shown inside to be less of a draw, but the outside art and grounds are reason enough to see this place.

THE SCULPTURE GARDEN

Giacometti's rough-hewn sculptures cast shadows across the courtyard. Although in his youth he sculpted classical busts with ease, as he got older, Giacometti repeatedly reworked and reduced his figures to almost nothing.

Aimé Maeght invited Spanish architect Josep Lluís Sert to design the foundation's building and grounds after seeing the Barcelona studio Sert had created for Miró. Aimé worked closely with Sert and the artists themselves to determine not only the placement for each work of art but also what art should be created. This allowed the artists a rare opportunity to consider their art in the context of the Mediterranean environment.

Sert constructed the space using elements of a traditional Mediterranean village—white buildings, fluid indoor-outdoor spaces, abundant patios and courtyards, small passages, dense plantings, a personal, human scale—and reinterpreted them in a modern way. The layout encourages you to wander, to digest, and to think; visitors are not crowded on top of one another but have many places to escape to with their thoughts.

The café is located near the entrance in a small stone building seemingly emerging from the landscape. It's a modest affair, but it has what you need. The chairs, tables, stools, and lamps were all designed by Giacometti.

A tiled reflecting pool

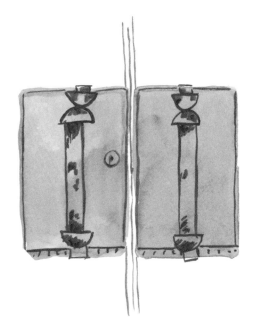

Brass door
handles by
Giacometti

A Giacometti sculpture

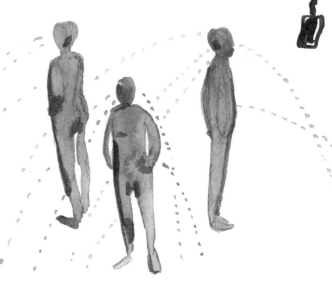

Sculptures in the
reflecting pool

BRAQUE'S MOSAIC POOL

Braque spent every January and February in Saint-Paul-de-Vence and was a dear friend of the Maeghts'. After they lost their young son, Bernard, to leukemia, it was Braque who encouraged them to start the foundation. He thought creating something beyond themselves would provide a respite from the pain they were in.

Braque had a lifelong interest in Cubism, and breaking things down helped him understand what he was representing. It is fitting that his last work was the foundation's mosaic pool. Sadly, he died in 1963, shortly before the inauguration of the foundation.

"Les Poissons,"
a mosaic pool
by Braque

Joan Miró, a Surrealist and one of Barcelona's best-known artists, created 250 works for the entrance courtyard, mostly sculptures and ceramics, representing a labyrinth through the artist's mind. He was opposed to traditional painting methods and enjoyed journeys into the subconscious. He enlisted the help of two ceramicists to produce the sculptures on display here.

"Fraul"

A Miró sculpture in the garden

Miró's fountain sculpture

" The Caress of a Bird "

HÔTEL LES VERGERS DE SAINT-PAUL

A ten-minute walk south of the Maeght Foundation on route de la Colle is the elegant fifteen-room Hôtel les Vergers de Saint-Paul. It's the area's best-kept secret and where I always stay. The rooms are arranged around the pool, and some even have their own ground-floor patios with retractable awnings, perfect to sit under while enjoying a morning café au lait.

At €160 a night, the rooms are a bargain for this area, and they're decorated beautifully, top to bottom, in yards of blue ticking fabric.

Vence

THE HILLTOP VILLAGE OF

VENCE,

formerly an ancient Roman settlement, is a ten-minute drive north of Saint-Paul-de-Vence. While some travelers may bypass it altogether in favor of the more storied Saint-Paul, I love visiting the scenic Old Town and Matisse's Chapel of the Rosary. I also love the more practical and down-to-earth essence of Vence. It looks and feels more real than some of the glossier towns in the region and combines the most authentic elements of the Riviera and Provence. On market days, residents and visitors alike can buy everything from fresh flowers and plants to cheese and eggs, and then wind their way through the narrow Old Town alleys to find a sundress or a tablecloth. Meanwhile, the landscape and light are just as inspiring as what you'd find in Nice or Antibes. Matisse, Dufy, Soutine, Chagall, and Delaunay came here often to paint among the olive and citrus trees, and Vence continues to attract many painters, writers, and sculptors to this day.

A good place to start a visit of the Old Town is in one of its main squares: place du Grand Jardin. Have a drink at Henry's, then walk the short distance to the heart of the square, where a handful of vendors sell locally sourced seasonal fruits and vegetables every day from 9:00 a.m. to 1:00 p.m. There are some fabulous plane trees that provide a broad, leafy canopy and relief from the midday sun.

On Friday mornings, the Marché du Pays Vençois brings a more expansive selection of local products to town. Vendors set up their tables along rue du Marché, inside the medieval walls, all the way through to place du Grand Jardin. As is the case with many big Provençal markets, you can spend all morning here, stocking up for a week's worth of meals. Under the shade of colorful umbrellas, mouthwatering displays of locally sourced meats, jams, and fresh produce are for sale. Permanent shopkeepers get in on the action by opening their doors to the street.

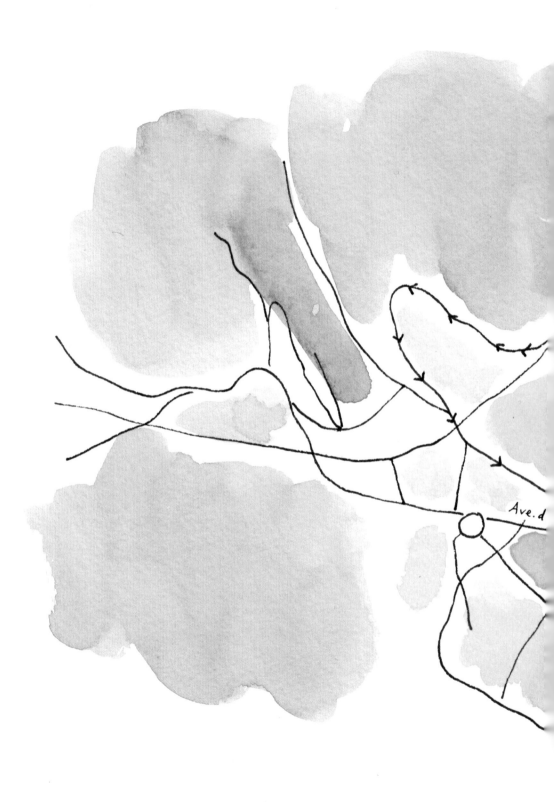

Ave. d

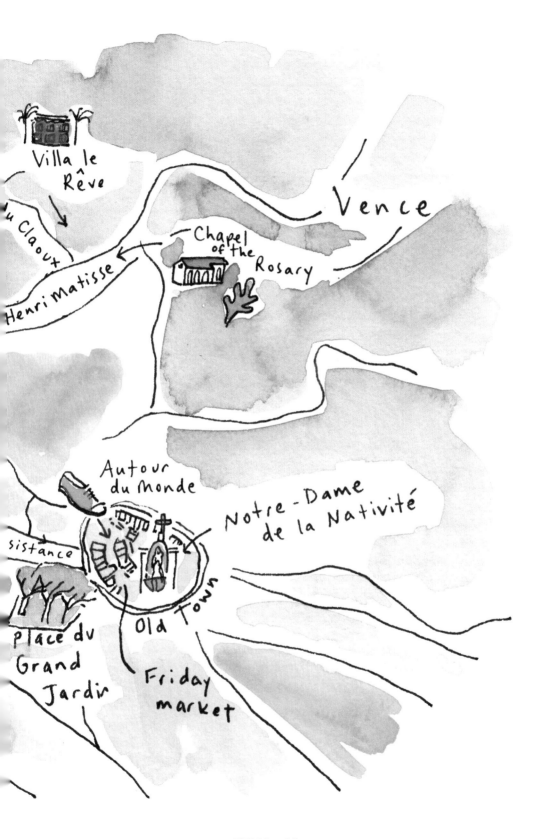

Villa le Rêve

u Claoux

Henri Matisse

Chapel of the Rosary

Vence

Autour du Monde

Notre-Dame de la Nativité

sistance

Place du Grand Jardin

Old Town

Friday market

PROVENÇAL FABRICS

Vence is a good place to buy classic Provençal fabrics. Inside the Old Town walls, you'll find stores that sell everything from olive-print tablecloths with matching quilted place mats to lavender sachets and vibrant ruffled dresses for little girls.

In the seventeenth century, Provence was flooded with imports of colorful block-printed textiles from India. The East India Company had just been established, and its merchant ships brought the goods to Marseille duty-free. Fabric-printing workshops were set up in Marseille, Arles, Avignon, and Nîmes, and cheerful cotton fabrics soon became synonymous with Provençal style.

Easter festivities in Vence include a three-day-long celebration during which locals dress up in straw hats and full-skirted traditional Provençal costumes. Dancers, baton twirlers, and musicians perform on the streets of the Old Town, and at the Notre-Dame de la Nativité cathedral, traditional Easter Sunday Mass is followed by a ceremony to crown the Queen of Vence. Easter Monday brings the Big Queen's Parade (Grand Corso de la Reine), a procession of flower-festooned floats that wind through the streets and compete for best floral decoration prize.

To see more Provençal textiles, visit the Provençal Museum of Costume and Jewelry in Grasse, a forty-minute drive away.

"LA TENNIS" BENSIMON

The iconic "la tennis" Bensimon canvas-and-rubber sneakers have long been staples in the French wardrobe, especially along the Riviera. They come in bright colors and are made out of 100 percent natural fabrics and rubber. My favorites are the slip-on kind (€30). They are sold in Autour du Monde, off the main square, along with a gorgeous selection of boho tunics, scarves, and bags in various colors and prints.

Villa le Rêve

Chemin du Claoux

Ave. Henri Matisse

← town square

Chapel of the Rosary

Vence

VILLA LE RÊVE

Henri Matisse lived at Villa le Rêve, up on a hill, from 1944 to 1948. Although his roots were in northern France, Matisse left his wife and children in 1917 to live by himself in the Nice suburb of Cimiez (see page 56). He spent most of the next thirty-seven years on the Riviera, moving to Vence when the threat of aerial bombardment prompted his departure from Nice. At Villa le Rêve, he embarked upon one of the most prolific painting periods of his life.

Today, the villa is owned by the city of Vence and can be rented out to artists by the week (€3,028 per week for a maximum of twelve people). If you are passing through Vence, try contacting Madame Audry, the woman in charge of renting its rooms, and ask for a tour. It's a living piece of history and a unique opportunity to walk the same gardens that inspired Matisse, though its interiors, now dormitory-like bedrooms, have lost some of their charm.

In 1941, while Matisse was recovering from an operation in Nice, he hired a young nurse named Monique Bourgeois, who became his caregiver and part-time muse. In 1943, Bourgeois joined a Dominican convent in Vence and became Sister Jacques-Marie. She told Matisse of the convent's plans to build a chapel, and in return for her kindness and care, he offered to design a stained-glass window. Eventually, he decided to design the whole structure, giving him complete artistic control, from the windows to the rooftop tiles and liturgical vestments.

Matisse and Sister Jacques-Marie

THEN AND NOW

During his time at the villa, Matisse often featured the palm trees outside his first-floor studio in his paintings. Now, seventy years later, the palms tower over the house.

THE CHAPEL OF THE ROSARY

Matisse considered the Chapel of the Rosary his crowning achievement. Built between 1949 and 1951, it's a small, spartan structure flooded with blue and yellow light from the stained-glass windows.

Fellow atheist, friend, and rival Picasso was horrified. "Picasso was furious that I'm doing a church," Matisse wrote. While there may have been some jealousy at play, Picasso was still supportive of his friend, introducing him to ceramicists to help execute his drawings on tile. A year after the chapel was completed, Picasso created his own murals to decorate a small chapel in Vallauris.

The Chapel of the Rosary operates as a place of worship, and it usually closes at lunchtime, so check the hours before visiting.

Matisse's *Chapelle du Rosaire des Dominicaines de Vence*, an account of his work on the chapel, sells for $1,700 at the Manhattan Rare Book Company.

The stained-glass windows behind the altar were designed using blue, green, and yellow in Matisse's iconic "sheaf" motif.

THE CHASUBLES

Matisse designed stunning liturgical vestments in vivid colors and with simple, cutout motifs for the priests to wear. The original chasubles are still housed in the Chapel of the Rosary, but duplicates made by the nuns are on display at the Vatican's modern religious art museum in Rome. It's also worth a visit to the Centre Pompidou in Paris: Matisse's original maquettes (paper models) of the vestments are all housed there.

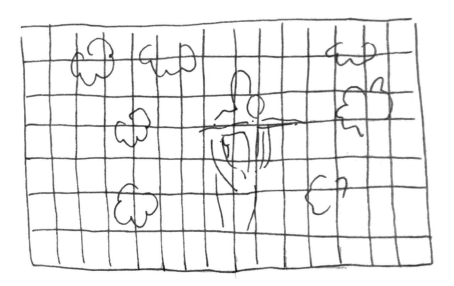

THE MURALS

Matisse created the chapel's three murals—*Saint Dominic*, *The Virgin Mother and Child*, and *The Stations of the Cross*— while in a chair. He fastened a brush or a piece of charcoal to the end of a stick and sketched out his designs on the wall. Later, local craftsmen transferred the drawings to white tiles, which were then installed on the interior walls.

Antibes

WITH ITS PROMINENT CLIFF-
TOP PERCH, SANDY BEACHES,
AND YACHT-FILLED MARINA,

ANTIBES

is a popular town on the coastal road between Cannes
and Nice. The ancient Greeks were the first to settle here,
calling it Antipolis ("counter-city" in Greek); much later,
such notables as painter Paul Signac and novelists Graham
Greene and Jules Verne found inspiration in the landscape
and the once-quiet cobblestoned Old Town. To the south

is Cap d'Antibes, an exclusive enclave that's blanketed with pine forests and luxurious villas, one of which was home to F. Scott Fitzgerald, his wife, Zelda, and their daughter, Scottie. Its famously secluded Hotel du Cap-Eden-Roc inspired the setting for Fitzgerald's *Tender Is the Night*.

While today the tourists may outnumber the famous locals, the city's thousand-year-old ramparts are a reminder of its storied history as a trading post and military stronghold. In the historic Old Town, an easy ten-minute walk from the train station, there are some worthwhile stops for food and drink, and some of the area's best beaches are not far away. To get there, follow the waterfront promenade all the way, passing the port and its yachts on your left.

Vallauris

Château de Vallauris

former site of madoura Workshop

train
station

Old
Port

Plage
de la Gravette

Amareno

Antibes

Jean-Luc
Pelé

Picasso
Museum

Old Town

Plage du
Ponteil

Plage de la
Salis

Juan-les-
Pins

Plage de la Garoupe

Cap
d'Antibes

coastal
path

Hotel du Cap-
Eden-Roc

THE PLANT AND FLOWER MARKET

If you're lucky, you may run into the city's plant
and flower market. It's situated along avenue de
Verdun, just before it enters the Old Town, in a
pretty square that's packed with typical Riviera plant
life—clementines, kumquats, and lemon trees, to
name a few. Fragrant and eye-catching, they are all
for sale and seemingly begging to be planted in a
beautiful seaside garden.

Try an authentic gelato at Amarena on rue Thuret. The lemon and mint flavors are out of this world.

THE OLD TOWN

At the heart of the city, ringed by thick medieval walls, is the Old Town. Touristy shops sell the souvenirs, straw hats, and market bags that are ubiquitous in the South of France. Owned and run by Sicilian Bruno Sciacca, a second-generation *maître glacier*, Amarena offers gelato crafted from fresh, local ingredients. Although it can get crowded (especially after dinner), it's well worth the wait.

THE BEACHES

A short stroll from the train station, just beside the Old
Port, is Plage de la Gravette. Sheltered by ancient walls on
three sides and blessed with fine, soft white sand, the beach
is both scenic and convenient; expect it to be crowded in the
summer months. Farther afield, stretching in the direction
of Cap d'Antibes, you'll find Plage du Ponteil and Plage de
la Salis. One of the prettiest beaches in the region is Plage
de la Garoupe, the starting point of a scenic hiking trail
that runs around the edge of the cape. There are swimming
coves (don't forget to pack a bathing suit and water shoes)
and a footpath made more interesting by an uneven terrain
of stairs, rocks, and old tree trunks.

PÂTISSERIE

In France, pastry chefs are like rock stars. They are alchemist, painter, and sculptor all in one, experimenting with flavors, colors, and textures and creating works that are both beautiful and delicious. Use of the term *pâtisserie* is strictly regulated in France and refers both to the pastries and the place where you buy them. Only a licensed *maître pâtissier* can own and run one. Walk into an authentic pâtisserie and you'll be tempted by an exquisite selection that might include éclairs, macarons, madeleines, cakes, and truffles. Fruit tarts are a summer specialty.

My favorite pâtisserie in Antibes is Jean-Luc Pelé. Jean-Luc himself is a local legend. He owns four shops in Antibes and Cannes and specializes in creamy éclairs, decadent chocolates, and mouthwatering macarons. Shaped like soft clouds, macarons quite literally melt in your mouth. His unusual flavors include everything from foie gras and crème brûlée to Nutella; they'll have you saying *"Miam-miam!"* like a local.

THE PICASSO MUSEUM

In 1946, the city of Antibes offered Picasso a six-month stay at Grimaldi Castle in return for some of his works. This spectacular château is where his namesake museum is now located. The Picasso Museum does not house his most famous paintings but rather a small collection on the third floor in what was his former studio. There is an entire wall devoted to his ceramic plates. The remaining floors feature rotating exhibits of other artists' work.

The main reason I visit the museum is to see the château and to take in the panoramic views from its terrace, which is lined with sculptures by various artists. Built of sand-colored stones on top of the remnants of ancient Greek foundations, the former fort was home to the Grimaldi family beginning in the early 1600s and became the town hall in 1702. The ancient structure juts out dramatically over the cliffs like the bow of a ship, and wherever you look, there's a stunning Mediterranean vista to take in.

A view from the museum's terrace

Cacti and terra-cotta pots on the terrace

THE MADOURA WORKSHOP

Nearby Vallauris is known as the "City of Clay" for its studios that carry on ceramic traditions dating back to Roman times. The city's reputation was given a giant boost when Picasso took up residence at the Madoura workshop from 1948 to 1955.

In 1946, Picasso saw a pottery exhibition displaying some of Madoura's work. He introduced himself to the owners, and they offered him some studio space and set out to teach him everything they knew. He was sixty-six years old.

For the next seven years, Picasso churned out hundreds of ceramic pieces with the help of his fellow potters. He started with simple plates and bowls and later made vases, jugs, sculptures, and plaques. The Madoura family had exclusive rights to reproduce and sell Picasso's work; by his death, that numbered 633 original designs, which they produced in editions of up to 500 each. The Madoura/Picasso partnership would last a quarter of a century. So inspiring were his creations that Matisse and Chagall began visiting the workshop to make their own pieces in clay. The legacy of Picasso's work here was a new movement of artists and craftspeople working together.

Madoura continued producing Picasso's editions until it closed its doors in 2007. To see more Picasso art on display, visit the Château de Vallauris. Its three small museums include a chapel that houses eighteen paintings Picasso created in 1952. They are collectively known as "War and Peace."

"Owl"

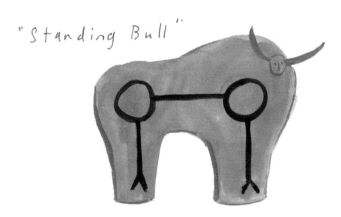

"Standing Bull"

"Female Faun"

PICASSO'S CERAMICS

Picasso was not trained as a ceramicist. This art form was new territory for him, and he approached it with a sense of freedom. His favorite subjects were bullfights, faces, owls, goats, birds, and fish.

For more complex shapes, Picasso sketched out unusual contours that played on traditional pottery vessels. He would upend them, contort them, and then hand the design to a craftsman to throw for him. Because he removed their function, the vessels became works of art rather than traditional, utilitarian ceramics. Picasso would then assemble the objects and paint them.

At the workshop, Picasso fell in love with a young assistant, Jacqueline Roque, whom he married in 1961. It was his second marriage. By then he'd already had four children with three different women, while keeping plenty of lovers on the sidelines. He and Jacqueline would eventually take a house at the foothills of Mont Sainte-Victoire, a Provençal mountain immortalized in a series of famous paintings by Cézanne. Picasso took great pleasure in owning the house, telling his dealer, "I bought the real Mont Sainte-Victoire!"

Picasso and Jacqueline are buried there at the Château de Vauvenargues. Jacqueline famously barred his three illegitimate children from attending their father's funeral and allegedly made sure they didn't receive a penny of his fortune.

Saint - Tropez

BRIGITTE BARDOT CAME TO

SAINT-TROPEZ

in the 1950s and transformed the peaceful fishing village
into a jet-set favorite overnight. Tropezians have thrived on
their sexy image ever since: in the summer, Saint-Tropez's
population of five thousand balloons to sixty thousand. At
the Old Port, yachts jostle for moorings and tourists jostle
to admire them. There is a serene side to this quaint village,
but it's best found in the low season. Meander cobbled lanes
in the old fishing quarter of La Ponche, sip pastis at a place
des Lices café, watch old men play *pétanque* beneath plane
trees, or walk in solitary splendor from beach to beach along
the coastal path.

Situated at the far western reaches of the Côte d'Azur, about an hour and a half's drive from Antibes and two hours from Nice, Saint-Tropez is the often-misunderstood, isolated fishing village with a glamorous, see-and-be-seen persona. It's more remote than the other towns of the Riviera, and heavy traffic (particularly in summer) makes it hard to get in and out. Take your time and enjoy the scenery. As you approach on a winding single-lane coastal road, a pastel-hued jewel will emerge from the surrounding verdant hills. Yachts and sailboats of all shapes and sizes (the largest look like cruise ships) are anchored in the turquoise-colored bay at the Old Port.

Cars are strictly verboten, so turn left into Parking du Nouveau Port at the town's entrance and explore lovely, walkable Saint-Tropez on foot. Head first to the Old Port, past the yachts and cafés, down the cobbled shopping streets, and take in the views of the pink buildings and the towering bell tower. It's a pretty, pretty town. The beaches are a little farther away, along the Bay of Pampelonne, and you'll need a car to get there.

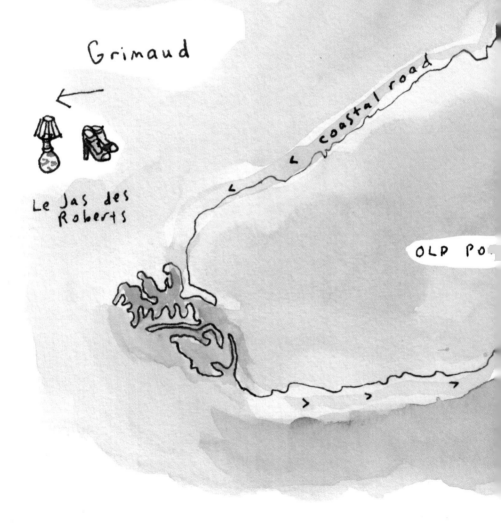

Grimaud

Le Jas des
Roberts

coastal road

OLD PO.

Sainte-
Maxine

Saint-
Tropez

Annonciade
Museum

ages
Lices . Bla Bla
Rondini

OLD TOWN

beaches

BLA BLA

....

Situated just two blocks from the port, Bla Bla is a gem of
a boutique with the feel of an exotic bazaar. Walk through
a tiny courtyard into a vaulted cave to find a bohemian
paradise. Owners Viviane Vidal de la Blache and Marie-
Christine Blanc have created their own universe filled with
dreamy tunics, flowy caftans, bikinis, scarves, straw hats,
and dresses from independent designers around the world.
These are clothes for sun lovers, clothes for the good life.

Orange
Crepe tunic

Mint bikini

Voile peasant blouse

Raspberry sundress

RONDINI

A block from Bla Bla, on rue Georges Clemenceau, you'll find Rondini, a family-run sandal shop that has been outfitting the feet of locals since 1927. The Rondini family proudly operates the oldest boutique in Saint-Tropez, and it's one of the few independent stores left. All of the sandals are made by hand, as they always have been, in the workshop behind the store. The craftsmen can make repairs or customize strap lengths to your specifications.

THE ANNONCIADE MUSEUM

....

On the edge of the Old Port is the Annonciade Museum, home to a surprisingly remarkable selection of Impressionist works and without the long lines you find at Paris museums. In the late 1800s, Paul Signac was taken with the light in this small village and word soon spread to Matisse, Dufy, Derain, and Bonnard. Their works are all represented here; most are paintings of Saint-Tropez.

THE OLD PORT

The Old Port is the center of town, a hub for people coming in and going out by boat or car or on foot, and it is lined with overpriced restaurants and cafés. It's a good place to sit and watch the action. Make sure to try a *tarte tropézienne* at one of Saint-Tropez's many bakeries.

BROCANTE DU JAS DES ROBERTS

There's a small flea market in Saint-Tropez on Tuesday and Saturday mornings, but it doesn't compare to Le Jas des Roberts in nearby Grimaud, which is twenty minutes away by car. Simply turn up the long driveway and park your car on the grass. Open only on Sundays, and spanning several farmers' fields, it is one of the best and largest flea markets on the Riviera.

You'll find everything from embroidered table linens to printed Sonia Rykiel dresses from the seventies to pendant lamps with milk-glass flanges from a hundred years ago. It takes hours to get through everything, so plan to get there early in the morning.

At the far end of the market, there's a lovely terraced café for lunch. It can get very crowded, so I sometimes sneak into the kitchen and ask the chef to sell me a sandwich.

Yellow, ball-shaped
clip-on earrings like
my grandmother wore

1930s navy and white spectator pumps

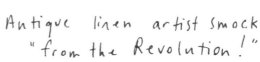

Antique linen artist smock "from the Revolution!"

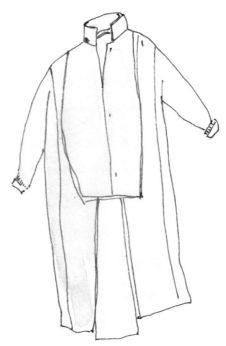

A set of twelve antique embroidered cloth napkins

Embellished mugs with lids

Au revoir,
Saint-Tropez!

WHAT to BRING
with YOU...

• • •

In the past few years, I've started bringing my art supplies with me when I travel. It has transformed my trips, forcing me to choose my itinerary with painting in mind and to set aside quiet time to take in the surroundings.

WATERCOLORS

• A watercolor set by Schmincke or Winsor & Newton, or make your own palette

• Brushes

• A bottle of water

• Paper towels

• A watercolor paper pad to rest on your lap

ACRYLICS

• Acrylic paints

• A paper palette

• Brushes

• A bottle of water

• A palette knife for mixing

• Retarder for extending paint life by an hour or two

• A rag

• An apron

• Canvas

• A collapsible easel and a stool (optional)

(Oils are not ideal for travel unless you are staying in one spot for a week because they take so long to dry.)

and WHAT to BRING HOME

• • •

Leaving the South of France is never easy, but there are plenty of things you can bring home to remind you of your time here.

- Bensimon sneakers

- Large packages of lavender for filling your own hand-sewn pillows at home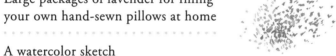

- A watercolor sketch

- A black stone from the beach in Nice

- Anything from Monoprix

- Roger & Gallet soap from the pharmacy

- A pair of espadrilles

- Perfume from Fragonard

- Paints or a sketchbook from Charvin

- An issue of the popular home décor magazine *Côté Sud*

WHERE to
EAT, STAY, and
EXPLORE

• • •

ANTIBES

AMARENA

....

18 rue Thuret, 06600

+33 6 01 06 14 38

gelateria-amarena.com

Open daily from
9:00 a.m. to 11:30 p.m.

JEAN-LUC PELÉ

....

27 rue de la République, 06600

+33 4 92 95 78 21

jeanlucpele.com/fr/adresse

Open daily from
9:00 a.m. to 7:30 p.m.

PICASSO MUSEUM

....

Grimaldi Castle

Place Mariejol, 06600

+33 4 92 90 54 28

antibesjuanlespins.com/en/
art-et-culture/picasso-museum

Open Tuesday through Sunday from
10:00 a.m. to 1:00 p.m. and from 2:00
to 6:00 p.m., except January 1, May 1,
November 1, and December 25.

GRASSE

PROVENÇAL MUSEUM OF
COSTUME AND JEWELRY

....

2 rue Jean Ossola, 06130

+33 4 93 36 44 65

fragonard.com/fr/usines/
musee-du-costume

Open daily from
10:00 a.m. to 1:00 p.m.
and from 2:00 to 6:30 p.m.
Closed Sunday in November,
January, and early February.

MENTON

ANNONCIADE MONASTERY

....

2135 corniche André Tardieu, 06500

+33 4 93 35 76 92

menton.fr/Monastere-de-l-
Annonciade.html

Open in summer daily from
8:00 a.m. to 7:00 p.m.; in winter
daily from 8:00 a.m. to 6:00 p.m.

JEAN COCTEAU MUSEUM

2 quai de Monléon, 06500

+33 4 89 81 52 50

museecocteaumenton.fr

Open Wednesday through
Monday from 10:00 a.m. to
6:00 p.m.

OLD CHÂTEAU CEMETERY

Rue du Vieux-Château, 06500

+33 4 92 10 50 00

Call for visiting hours.

SAINT-MICHEL BASILICA

Parvis Saint-Michel, 06500

+33 4 93 35 81 63

paroissedementon.fr//21/5/2/
basilique-saint-michel-archange.html

Open Monday through Friday from
10:00 a.m. to noon and from
3:00 to 5:00 p.m.; Saturday and
Sunday from 3:00 to 5:00 p.m.

SALLE DES MARIAGES

17 rue de la République, 06500

+33 4 92 10 50 00

Open Monday through Friday from
8:30 a.m. to noon and from
2:00 to 4:30 p.m.

NICE

ANTIQUES MARKET

Cours Saleya, 06300

en.nicetourisme.com/nice/1398-
marche-a-la-brocante-saleya

Open Monday from
7:00 a.m. to 6:00 p.m.

ARÈNES DE CIMIEZ (ROMAN AMPHITHEATER)

Avenue des Arènes de Cimiez, 06000

+33 4 93 81 08 08

Gardens open in July and August
daily from 8:00 a.m. to 8:00 p.m.;
September to June daily from
8:00 a.m. to 6:00 p.m.

CHAGALL MUSEUM

36 avenue Docteur Ménard,
06000

+33 4 93 53 87 20

en.musees-nationaux-alpesmaritimes
.fr/chagall

Open May through October
Wednesday through Monday
from 10:00 a.m. to 6:00 p.m.;
November through April Wednesday
through Monday
from 10:00 a.m. to 5:00 p.m.

CHARVIN

39 rue Gioffredo, 06000

+33 4 93 92 92 82

charvin-arts.com

Open Monday through Saturday
from 9:00 a.m. to 7:00 p.m.

CIMIEZ MONASTERY

Place Jean-Paul II, 06000

+33 4 93 81 00 04

Church open Monday through
Saturday from 9:15 a.m. to
6:00 p.m. and Sunday from noon
to 6:00 p.m.; closed Wednesday
mornings and during services.
Museum open Monday through
Saturday from 10:00 a.m. to noon
and from 3:00 to 5:30 p.m.
Small cloister open daily from
9:15 a.m. to 5:30 p.m.

FLOWER AND PRODUCE MARKETS

Cours Saleya, 06300

+33 4 92 14 46 14

en.nicetourisme.com/markets

Flower Market open Tuesday through Saturday from 6:00 a.m. to 5:30 p.m.; Sunday from 6:30 a.m. to 1:30 p.m.

Produce Market open Tuesday through Sunday from 6:00 a.m. to 1:00 p.m.

MATISSE MUSEUM

164 avenue des Arènes de Cimiez, 06000

+33 4 93 81 08 08

musee-matisse-nice.org

Open June 23 to October 15 Wednesday through Monday from 10:00 a.m. to 6:00 p.m.; October 16 to June 22 Wednesday through Monday from 11:00 a.m. to 6:00 p.m.

MONOPRIX

Locations throughout the city

0 800 08 4000

monoprix.fr

Hours vary by location.

MUSEUM OF MODERN AND CONTEMPORARY ART

Place Yves Klein, 06364

+33 4 97 13 42 01

mamac-nice.org

Open June 23 to October 15 Tuesday through Sunday from 10:00 a.m. to 6:00 p.m.; October 16 to June 22 Tuesday through Sunday from 11:00 a.m. to 6:00 p.m. Call for special night hours.

LE PATIO AT HÔTEL LA PÉROUSE

11 quai Rauba Capeù, 06300

+33 4 93 62 34 63

hotel-la-perouse.com/en/page/ restaurant-bar.45.html

Open daily from 7:00 to 11:00 a.m., noon to 2:00 p.m., and 7:00 to 10:00 p.m. (7:00 to 9:00 p.m. in winter).

RÉGINA PALACE

71 boulevard de Cimiez, 06000

Closed to the public.

SAINT-JEAN-CAP-FERRAT

GRAND-HÔTEL DU CAP-FERRAT

71 boulevard du Général de Gaulle, 06230

+33 4 93 76 50 50

fourseasons.com/capferrat

The hotel is closed each winter from December to February. Club Dauphin is open from May 26 to October 1 daily from 12:30 to 4:30 p.m. (until 5:00 p.m. in July and August).

LIGHTHOUSE

Chemin du Phare, 06230

Closed to the public.

VILLA EPHRUSSI

1 avenue Ephrussi de Rothschild, 06230

+33 4 93 01 33 09

villa-ephrussi.com/en

Open July and August daily from
10:00 a.m. to 7:00 p.m.; November
through January Monday through
Friday from 2:00 to 6:00 p.m.,
Saturday and Sunday from
10:00 a.m. to 6:00 p.m.; rest of
the year daily from 10:00 a.m.
to 6:00 p.m.

Tearoom open February through
October daily from 11:00 a.m. to
5:30 p.m.; November through
January only on weekends and
holidays.

VILLA SANTO SOSPIR

14 avenue Jean Cocteau, 06230

santosospir.com

Open by appointment only:
contact Éric Marteau at
+33 4 93 76 00 16 or
visits@santosospir.com

SAINT-PAUL-DE-VENCE

CAFÉ DE LA PLACE

1 place du Général de Gaulle, 06570

+33 4 93 32 80 03

Open in summer daily from
7:00 a.m. to midnight; in winter
from 7:00 a.m. to 8:00 p.m.
Closed in November and December.

LA COLOMBE D'OR

1 place du Général de Gaulle, 06570

+33 4 93 32 80 02

la-colombe-dor.com

Restaurant open daily from
12:30 to 2:00 p.m. and from
7:30 to 10:00 p.m. Open for
breakfast for hotel guests only from
7:30 to 10:30 a.m. The hotel and
restaurant are closed from November
to just before Christmas.

LA CURE GOURMANDE

23 rue Grande, 06570

+33 4 93 32 16 96

curegourmande.com/
la-cure-gourmande-st-paul-de-vence

Open daily from
9:30 a.m. to 7:00 p.m.

FRAGONARD

Chemin de Sainte-Claire, 06570

+33 4 93 58 58 58

fragonard.com/fr/boutique/
saint-paul-de-vence

Open daily from
9:30 a.m. to 6:00 p.m.

HÔTEL LES VERGERS
DE SAINT-PAUL

940 route de la Colle, 06570

+33 4 93 32 94 24

lesvergersdesaintpaul.com

Open year-round.

LILAS BOHÈME

26 rue Grande, 06570

+33 4 93 59 77 82

bohemeenprovence.com

Call for hours.

MAEGHT FOUNDATION

623 chemin des Gardettes, 06570

+33 4 93 32 81 63

fondation-maeght.com

Open daily July through September
from 10:00 a.m. to 7:00 p.m.;
October through June from
10:00 a.m. to 6:00 p.m.

Le Café F hours change seasonally.
Call + 33 4 93 32 45 96 for details.

MAISON BRÉMOND

28 rue Grande, 06570

+33 4 93 58 07 69

Open Monday through Friday from
10:00 a.m. to 1:30 p.m. and from
2:00 to 6:30 p.m.

SAINT-TROPEZ

ANNONCIADE MUSEUM

2 rue de l'Annonciade, place Georges
Grammont, 83990

+33 4 94 17 84 10

saint-tropez.fr/fr/culture/
musee-de-lannonciade

Open Tuesday through Sunday
from 10:00 a.m. to 1:00 p.m. and
from 2:00 to 6:00 p.m.; closed in
November.

BLA BLA

3 place de la Garonne, 83990

+33 4 94 97 45 09

Open April through October daily
from 10:00 a.m. to 8:00 p.m.; in
March Friday through Tuesday from
10:30 a.m. to 1:30 p.m. and from
3:00 to 6:00 p.m.; closed November
through February.

BROCANTE DU JAS DES ROBERTS

RD14, 83310, Grimaud

+33 6 67 71 74 27

facebook.com/pg/
brocantedujasdesroberts

Open Sunday from
7:00 a.m. to 1:00 p.m.

RONDINI

18 rue Georges Clemenceau, 83990

+33 4 94 97 19 55

rondini.fr

Open in summer (roughly from
Easter through October) daily
from 9:30 a.m. to 12:30 p.m. and
from 2:00 to 6:30 p.m.; in winter
(November through March)
Tuesday through Saturday from
10:30 a.m. to 12:30 p.m. and from
3:00 to 6:30 p.m.

VALLAURIS

CHÂTEAU DE VALLAURIS: MUSÉE NATIONAL PABLO PICASSO

Place de la Libération, 06220

+33 4 93 64 71 83

en.musees-nationaux-alpesmaritimes
.fr/picasso

Open in July and August daily from
10:00 a.m. to 12:45 p.m. and
from 2:15 to 6:15 p.m.; in September
Wednesday through Monday from
10 a.m. to 12:15 p.m. and from
2:00 to 5:00 p.m.

VENCE

AUTOUR DU MONDE

4 place du Peyra, 06140

+33 4 93 24 08 42

bensimon.com/fr_fr/vence-autour-du-monde-83.html

Open Tuesday through Saturday
from 11 a.m. to 1:00 p.m. and
from 2:30 to 7 p.m.

CHAPEL OF THE ROSARY

466 avenue Henri Matisse, 06141

+33 4 93 58 03 26

chapellematisse.com

Open April 1 to October 31 Tuesday,
Thursday, and Friday from
10:00 a.m. to noon and from
2:00 to 6:00 p.m.; Wednesday and
Saturday from 2:00 to 6:00 p.m.
Open November 1 to March 31
Tuesday, Thursday, and Friday from
10:00 a.m. to noon and from
2:00 to 5:00 p.m.; Wednesday and
Saturday from 2:00 to 5:00 p.m.

HENRY'S BAR

48 avenue Marcellin Maurel, 06140

+33 4 93 58 67 83

Open Thursday through Tuesday
from 6:30 a.m. to 9:00 p.m.

FRUIT AND VEGETABLE MARKET

Place du Grand-Jardin, 06140

+33 4 93 58 40 16

vence-tourisme.com/en/markets

Open Tuesday through Sunday from
9:00 a.m. to 1:00 p.m.

MARCHÉ DU PAYS VENÇOIS

Place du Grand Jardin, 06140

+33 4 93 58 40 16

vence-tourisme.com/en/markets

Open Friday from
9:00 a.m. to 1:00 p.m.

NOTRE-DAME DE LA NATIVITÉ CATHEDRAL

Place Clemenceau, 06140

+33 4 93 58 42 00

vence.fr/our-lady-of-nativity

Open daily from
9:00 a.m. to 6:00 p.m.

VILLA LE RÊVE

261 avenue Henri Matisse, 06140

+33 6 37 74 86 91

villalerevevence.com

ACKNOWLEDGMENTS

• • •

A big thank-you to my parents for encouraging my artistic journeys, and to my children, who astonish me every day with their creations. I'm lucky that my husband understands my love of travel and uncomplainingly assumed extra parenting duties so I could research this book.

Somehow my siblings and I have managed to meet up in France every few years despite our busy, adult lives, and I'm grateful that they're always up for a trip somewhere.

I'm thankful to Stephanie Pesakoff for all the enthusiasm she's shown for my work over the years, and for introducing me to Lia Ronnen at Artisan, who turned out to be the perfect publisher. Thanks also to Shoshana Gutmajer, my thorough and patient editor, and to the design team, Raphael Geroni, Michelle Ishay, and Jane Treuhaft, for working hard to get it just right. I'm indebted to my childhood friend Mercedeh Sanati for stepping in at the eleventh hour and adding her energy and beauty to my words. I'm also grateful to Deborah Needleman, who introduced me to the wonders of Madeleine Castaing when I illustrated her book.

And lastly, I'm indebted to my grandparents Anne and Alex, whose adventurous stories—told to me at bedtime—of their travels before, during, and after the war inspire me long after they're gone.